PICTURES
AND
POLLUTION

By
Barbara
Slavin
Kataoka

12,246

CHILDRENS PRESS,

CHICAGO

For Mother and Clyde

Cover picture: *The Waterfall* by Henri-Julien Rousseau. 1910. Oil on Canvas. 45½ in. by 59 in. Courtesy of The Art Institute of Chicago, Helen Birch Bartlett Memorial Collection.
Frontis: *Sunday Afternoon on the Island of La Grande Jatte* by Georges Seurat. 1884-86. Oil on Canvas. 81 in. by 120¾ in. Courtesy of The Art Institute of Chicago, Helen Birch Bartlett Memorial Collection.

Library of Congress Cataloging in Publication Data

Kataoka, Barbara Slavin.
    Pictures and pollution.

    SUMMARY: Discusses pollution and its effects as depicted in various works of art.
    1. Pollution—Juvenile literature. [1. Pollution]
I. Title.
TD176.K37   301.31   76-54136
ISBN 0-516-00559-6

CONTENTS

POLLUTION PROBLEMS

Pollution is a word you often hear and read about.

Pollution may harm the planet we live on. All living things can be hurt by pollution.

Artists care about pollution. Their pictures show that they care.

In this book you will have a chance to see some of these pictures.

Wheatfields by Jacob Isaaksz van Ruisdael
Oil on canvas. 39⅜ in. by 51¼. in.

Industrial Town by Vincent van Gogh

AIR POLLUTION

There are many kinds of pollution. This picture shows air pollution.

A Dutch artist painted it almost a hundred years ago. There were pollution problems then, too.

Clouds of black smoke rise from the smokestacks. The smoke pollutes the air.

Polluted air can damage our lungs. It can damage growing things. It can damage buildings, metal objects, and statues.

The problem of air pollution has become much worse since this picture was painted.

Automobiles cause the greatest amount of
air pollution in the United States.

The pollution comes from the gases that
pour out of the tailpipes of cars and trucks.
These gases poison the air.

Opposite page: *Standard Station, Amarillo, Texas,* by Edward Ruscha
1963. Oil on canvas. 65 in. by 121½ in.

This page: *Private Sanitation* by Ron Kleemann
44 in. by 66 in.

This page: *Friedrich Schiller* by Ernst Rau
Detail of face (left), full view (below).
Partially cleaned. In storage. Formerly
at St. Louis Park Place, St. Louis.
Dedicated 13 November 1898.

Opposite page: *Apotheosis of St. Louis* by
Charles Niehaus. Detail during cleaning
(top), full view, partially cleaned (bottom
Forest Park, St. Louis.
Dedicated 4 October 1906.

These pictures show the damage that air pollution can do to artwork. The statues you see here are being cleaned. There is a great difference between the parts of the statues that have been cleaned and the parts that are still dirty from air pollution.

The Mink Pond by Winslow Homer
1891. Watercolor. 13⅞ in. by 20 in.

WATER POLLUTION

Water pollution is caused by many things. Some factories dump their wastes into nearby waters.

Sewer pipes from some towns pour raw or nearly raw sewage into the waters.

People often throw trash into the waters.

Polluted waters may look ugly and dirty. They may even smell bad.

Today, many rivers and lakes are polluted. It is no longer safe to swim or fish there. Many of the fish in the waters are dying.

The people in these pictures are not fishing in polluted waters. They are fishing in clean waters. Since the times pictured here, many changes have taken place in rivers and lakes.

Opposite page, top: *The Manner of their Fishing* by John White

Opposite page, bottom: *Fishing and Fowling*
Egyptian Wall Painting
from Thebes, Tomb of Memena, Scribe of the Fields.
About 1415 B.C. 101 cm. by 189 cm.

This page: *Eel Spearing at Setauket* by William Sidney Mount

American Landscape by Charles Sheeler
1930. Oil on canvas. 24 in. by 31 in.

Towns and cities have grown up along
the waterways. People in the towns and cities
have polluted the waters. This picture shows
us one of the ways we pollute our waters.

June, 1882 by George Inness
Oil on canvas. 30¼ in. by 45 in.

WILDERNESS POLLUTION

The parts of our country that have been unspoiled by man are called wilderness areas. These areas have woods, grasslands, marshes, and wild animals.

Wilderness areas are valuable for many reasons. They are places where people may hike, camp, and enjoy nature. They are places where wild animals make their homes. The trees and green plants in these areas produce the oxygen that makes it possible for us to live.

This painting by Asher B. Durand shows the unspoiled wilderness of the Catskill Mountains in New York about a hundred years ago.

*Portrait
of Mao Mao*

The Hamlyn Group
Picture Library

It is important for us to save our
wilderness areas. When trees are cut down,
small animals and birds lose their homes.
Many kinds of animals that once lived do
not exist any more; they are extinct. Man has
destroyed their natural homes.

Much of the green land in our country
has been lost because we have built so many
roads and highways.

In our crowded cities, housing and
businesses have taken up most of the green
land that once was there.

Early Sunday Morning by Edward Hopper
1930. Oil on canvas. 35 in. by 60 in.

People in towns and cities need green, growing areas, too. That is why parks are important. Parks offer places of beauty for people to enjoy in all seasons.

These pictures show how people have enjoyed parks over the years.

Opposite page: *Skaters, Central Park* by William Glackens

This Page: *Central Park, 1901* by Maurice Prendergast
Watercolor. 14⅜ in. by 21½ in.

*Lower Manhattan (Composing
Derived from Top of Woolworth)*
by John Marin.
1922. Watercolor and charcoal
with paper cutout attached with
thread. 21⅝ in. by 26⅞ in.

Collection, The Museum of
Modern Art, New York.
Acquired through the
Lillie P. Bliss Bequest.

Broadway by Mark Tobey
Tempera on masonite board
26 in. by 19 3/16 in.

The Metropolitan Museum of Art.
Arthur H. Heard Fund, 1942.

NOISE POLLUTION AND VISUAL POLLUTION

Another kind of pollution is noise pollution. The two artists who painted the pictures on the opposite page showed a very crowded New York City. If you look closely, you might almost be able to hear the honking and other loud city noises.

You might also decide that these artists wanted to show still another kind of pollution—visual pollution. Sometimes the blinking lights and bright colors from city signs make you dizzy. This is visual pollution.

People who live in cities need parks. In a park they can rest their eyes and ears while they enjoy the natural beauty.

This painting by Ben Shahn shows some boys in a city playing the game of handball. In the playground there are no trees or grass. There are only ugly areas of concrete and pavement. This is a form of visual pollution.

Handball by Ben Shahn
1939. Tempera on paper over composition board.
22¾ in. by 31¼ in.

Mural for Boston's Orchard Park by Charles Milles

Even when there are no trees or grass or flowers around, there are some things that can be done to add beauty to our surroundings.

This is a picture of a handball court in Boston. Charles Milles painted a mural on this court. It is a mural of bold design and bright colors. The mural shows the contributions that black people have made to the fields of music, dance, and the theater. There is even a tree in the mural.

This is one way to change visual pollution to visual beauty.

LITTER

Some people have a careless habit. It is a habit that can spoil the beauty of the world around us.

Claes Oldenburg was thinking about this bad habit when he painted the picture you see here.

This picture shows litter.

Did you ever imagine what would happen to the world around you if all the litter, such as bits of paper, became larger and larger after they had been tossed aside?

In the picture the artist pretended that is what had happened.

What has happened to the rest of the space in the room?

Giant Fagends by Claes Oldenburg
1967. Canvas, urethane foam, and wood.
96 in. by 96 in. by 40 in.

Litter is a spoiler of the beauty in a room or on a street or lawn or anywhere in the community. That is why we should all take seriously the slogan, "Don't Be a Litterbug."

SAVE OUR PEOPLE

The artists whose pictures appear in this book have helped you think about problems of pollution.

You have learned some things about pollution, too.

Now you can see why the message on the poster at the right is an important one.

What *is* the message? What does the message mean to you?

Save Our Planet, Save Our People by Ernest Trova
Poster

About the Author:

Barbara Slavin Kataoka was born in a small Arizona town where she grew up to love the wide open spaces and clean crisp air of the Sonoran Desert. She majored in art history at Mt. Holyoke College in Massachusetts and continued her graduate studies in rural upstate New York at Cooperstown. In the Education Department at the Albright Knox Art Museum in Buffalo, she developed many special art programs for children. She has taught history and anthropology and has worked on a social science curriculum project for New York State. She is Vice Consul at the British Consulate-General at St. Louis. Mrs. Kataoka has traveled extensively throughout Europe, Southeast Asia, Australia, the South Pacific, and Japan. Currently she is writing another children's book on Energy and Art.